TYRELL WILLIAMS

Tyrell Williams is an award-winning writer and director for theatre, film and television. When initially presented at Bush Theatre in 2022, his first play *Red Pitch* – directed by Daniel Bailey – completed a sold-out run and Tyrell won the George Devine Award, The Stage Debut Award for Best Writer, Evening Standard Award for Most Promising Playwright, Critics' Circle Theatre Award for Most Promising Playwright and *Red Pitch* was awarded Best New Play at the OffWestEnd Awards 2023. *Red Pitch* is currently in development for a screen adaptation with Fudge Park. In addition to another original series he also has in development with Fudge Park, he has written an episode of an upcoming Apple TV+ series.

Tyrell has been named one of Deadline's five rising writers to watch in 2023, and is currently on attachment to the National Theatre Studio. In 2015, Tyrell co-created, co-wrote and directed the viral web series *#HoodDocumentary* which has had over four million views on YouTube. Following its online acclaim, *#HoodDocumentary* eventually went on to be commissioned for BBC Three which Tyrell directed and co-wrote. Tyrell was on the BAFTA Elevate scheme 2018 and was a Broadcast Hotshot in 2016.

Other Titles in this Series

Tyrell Williams

RED PITCH

NICK HERN BOOKS

London
www.nickhernbooks.co.uk

A Nick Hern Book

Red Pitch first published as a paperback original in Great Britain in 2022 by Nick Hern Books Limited, The Glasshouse, 49a Goldhawk Road, London W12 8QP, in association with the Bush Theatre

Reprinted with revisions 2022, 2023, 2024

Red Pitch © 2022, 2023, 2024 Tyrell Williams

Tyrell Williams has asserted his right to be identified as the author of this work

Cover photography by Helen Murray

Designed and typeset by Nick Hern Books, London
Printed in Great Britain by Mimeo Ltd, Huntingdon, Cambridgeshire PE29 6XX

A CIP catalogue record for this book is available from the British Library

ISBN   978 1 83904 349 9

www.nickhernbooks.co.uk/environmental-policy

Red Pitch was first performed at the Bush Theatre, London, on 16 February 2022, and revived on 7 September 2023. The production transferred to @sohoplace in London's West End on 16 March 2024, produced by Chuchu Nwagu, Eilene Davidson, Adam Kenwright and Nica Burns. The cast was as follows:

BILAL	Kedar Williams-Stirling
JOEY	Emeka Sesay
OMZ	Francis Lovehall

UNDERSTUDIES

JOEY/BILAL	Shem Hamilton
OMZ/BILAL	Toyin Omari-Kinch

Director	Daniel Bailey
Set & Costume Designer	Amelia Jane Hankin
Lighting Designer	Ali Hunter
Sound Designer	Khalil Madovi
Original Movement Director	Dickson Mbi
Movement Director	Gabrielle Nimo
Associate Director	Amber Ruby
Fight Director	Kev McCurdy
Costume Supervisor	Georgia Wilmot
Vocal Coach	Gurkiran Kaur
Football Consultant	Aaron Samuel
Casting Director	Heather Basten CDG

With thanks to: Lauren Clancy, Ricardo De Silva, Cockayne Grants, David Gregory, Mark Goucher, Cameron Bernard Jones, Wabriya King, Anelisa Lamola, Deirdre O'Halloran, Emily Mei-Ling Pearce, Madeleine Penfold, Playing Field, Monaé Robinson, Kala Simpson, Adam Spiegel, Andrew Treagus Associates.

Special thanks to:

Daniel L Bailey
Ann Akin
Ovalhouse Theatre
Titilola Dawudu
Toby Clarke
Michael Ajao
Ayomide Adegun
Ikky Elyaz
Montel Douglas
Malcolm Atobrah
Abdul Abdalla
Gamba Cole
Ivan Oyik
Imogen Sarre
Kirsten Foster
Joe Pierson

T.W.

'How they talking on what's threatening the economy?
Knocking down communities to re-up on properties'

Little Simz, 'Introvert'

Characters

BILAL AMARAL, *sixteen, male, Black*
OMZ (OMAR) RICHARDS, *sixteen, male, Black*
JOEY (JOSEPH) SESAY, *sixteen, male, Black*

Notes

The play is set in present-day 'urban' South London.

This story is taking place inside of a football pitch – 'Red Pitch'
– in summer.

There are scaffoldings around the football pitch.

A constant soundscape of construction underneath the piece
throughout its entirety is important to the telling of this story
and should be considered seriously in each production. The
soundscape of construction should at times feel literal, and at
other times abstract, representing the state of the friendship
between Bilal, Joey and Omz. It should be interspersed with a
protest pertaining to the survival of Esme's dry cleaner's that
begins innocuous, then grows in its potency but ultimately is
silenced. The specific sounds and journeys of the sounds are
decisions to be made at the director's discretion.

A dash (–) is used to indicate an interruption and a slash (/)
denotes an overlapping in dialogue.

Pauses and silences are important but are not fixed. Each pause
and silence should be considered in that moment. However,
more often than not, a silence should be longer than a pause.

Scene One

It's the summer holidays and there are two young friends,
BILAL and OMZ, playing football inside of a football pitch
whilst the third friend, JOEY, is attentively watching the game
whilst in goal. The game is FA.

BILAL and OMZ are really going for it. There is grabbing,
hard tackles flying in and sweat pouring from their faces.
Eventually, BILAL does his classic 'drop, drop' shoulder move
(a move in which he shifts his body weight to his right then to
his left then back to his right whilst tapping the ball in that
direction) taking him around OMZ. BILAL shoots and scores
a goal past JOEY, effectively ending the game.

BILAL remains humble in victory. OMZ is disappointed.

JOEY. Good shot bro.

BILAL. Light work.

JOEY. Mbappe yeah? Make sure you do that at the trials.

BILAL. Obviously. 'Drop, drop' shoulder – easy.

> *BILAL does the 'drop, drop' shoulder move again without*
> *the ball.*

> Omz, I want a tropical juice yeah.

> *OMZ pauses for a second, taken aback. He looks around as*
> *though BILAL could never be talking to him.*

OMZ. What?

BILAL. Tropical juice. It's a blue carton – says 'Sun Pride' on it.

OMZ. Why's that my problem?

JOEY. Here we go...

BILAL. Red Pitch rules: Loser of FA goes shop for the winner.
You lost. I won so pick me up a tropical juice... and a Twix.

JOEY. Let's just play *FIFA* you man.

OMZ *stands still staring at* BILAL.

BILAL. Bro, this isn't shop, this is Red Pitch.

OMZ. You cheated. You didn't / ask me if I was ready.

BILAL. / ask me if I was ready.

Pause.

OMZ. Wanna play best two / out of three?

BILAL. That was best two out of three.

OMZ. Joey / let it in.

JOEY. Nooo, I never.

OMZ. I'm not going nowhere. Where's Femi? We're supposed to be playing two-on-two anyway.

JOEY. Femi said he'd be down in twenty minutes when I knocked for him... (*Checking his phone.*) one hour and fifty-seven minutes ago.

OMZ. I bet you Femi's looking for that purple shirt. He loves wearing that purple shirt.

JOEY. Why does he wear it? Honestly, does he think it's cool?

BILAL. That shirt makes no sense. I can't lie.

OMZ. I think his brother got it for him.

BILAL. His brother set him up 'cause his brother's drip is on point, always.

JOEY. That's 'cause his brother is making big money. I think he does law – that's gonna be me soon, looking fly. (*Beat.*) It was sick when Femi's brother used to come Red Pitch.

BILAL. That was time ago.

OMZ. None of the olders come any more. (*Beat.*) You sure Femi's coming Joey?

JOEY. He said he was.

BILAL. You lot know that Femz is a liar. I remember knocking for this guy once, he said that he weren't allowed out, I said cool, okay, fair enough. It was winter them times and it was getting dark early or maybe he had a family commitment – whatever. I came Red Pitch now, worked on a few tekkers – can you believe next minute, I see him chilling in the park with his girl on the swings?

They all laugh.

OMZ. This guy.

BILAL. Swinging back and forth like this is a romcom!

OMZ. You should've went up to him.

BILAL. I did. He said that he couldn't play football 'cause he injured his leg when he was at work. He works in an office bro. Did he injure it making coffee?

They all laugh.

JOEY. Femi is setting pace though. He has a job, has a girlfriend at sixteen years old! They go on dates and everything.

BILAL. Psssh, sixteen is young man. We have time.

JOEY. So you man don't want a girl?! Someone you can take care of, someone to take care of you? You guys can be chilling, watching movies all cuddled up in bed on a cold day like today – eating popcorn in the warmth watching *Save the Last Dance*.

JOEY *imagines the scenario.*

'Hey, hey, hey, you have the last popcorn', 'No, you have it', 'Okay, we'll share it then.' You man saying you don't want that?!

BILAL. 'Save the Last' what?

JOEY. 'Dance' – it's some ooolllddd-school dance film. Litty though.

OMZ. Joseph, it's me: Omz. Do you know with whom that you speak with? I've had girls for days.

BILAL. Swear? What's their names?

OMZ. You lot don't know them.

JOEY. Try us.

> OMZ *gets the ball and then starts bouncing it.* BILAL *and* JOEY *wait.*

OMZ. Huh? Oh, you man still want names?

JOEY. You know we want names.

OMZ. Classified – that's their names.

> BILAL *and* JOEY *shake their heads.*

JOEY. Let's just play *FIFA* you man.

OMZ. We wait for Femz. We're meant to be playing two-on-two.

JOEY. It's like you love him.

OMZ. Dead! It'll be better practice for football trials.

BILAL. Ayyy! That's gonna be nuts! Professional football trials you know – I'm gonna be 'drop, drop' shouldering all over like…

> BILAL *demonstrates the 'drop, drop' shoulder move again.*

OMZ. Yeah, exactly but we need to practise, that's why Femz needs to be here. Can't be a professional footballer without putting in the work.

> *Silence.*

JOEY. It's cutting out 'ere man… Supposed to be summer you know? Climate change is real.

OMZ. Shake my head. You believe everything you hear on TikTok. Some any conspiracy theorist.

JOEY. I'm not you, you know.

OMZ. Bilz, ain't –

BILAL. Not involved bro. What's the point in saying we play and you're not even gonna follow through?

OMZ. What you talkin' 'bout?

BILAL. Shop – You're the one that said 'FA Red Pitch rules.'

JOEY. It's true though.

OMZ. Joey, stop bum-licking, man.

JOEY. I'm not bum-licking.

OMZ. You are.

JOEY. How? That's what you said though.

OMZ. So what? Ever since primary school days, you've always been defending Bilal like you're his lawyer. Why are you here in your jeans anyway? Rubbish footballer.

JOEY. I'm better than you and I'm just saying that's what you said. How is that bum-licking?

OMZ. Don't lie, doesn't he always stick up for you Bilal?

JOEY. Cap.

OMZ. And I've actually just deeped why you wanna 'go play *FIFA*' so much…

> OMZ *is more serious, ponderous even.* JOEY *waits.*

It's 'cause you're on lock.

> OMZ *laughs.*

JOEY. Capping.

OMZ. Bro! You know you're meant to be home right now Joey. You put your phone on silent so when your mum calls you, you think we won't clock it ringing but I see it with my eye. I'm just like 'Ohhh Boyyy… Home time.'

> JOEY *shakes his head.* BILAL *is ignoring* OMZ.

(*Still laughing.*) Bilz?!

BILAL. I'm not involved bro. All I know is Omar, you don't keep your word brother… 'And fulfil every engagement for every engagement will be enquired into the Day of Reckoning'…

OMZ. Agh whatever man!

OMZ *walks towards the exit.*

That pathetic reverse psychology. I swear if you man go – agh!

OMZ *sees the only football on his way out and takes it with him.*

BILAL (*shouting*). Tropical juice and a Twix.

OMZ *exits, ritualistically double-tapping the football cage on his way out.*

'Keeping your word' – works every time.

BILAL *goes to get his hooded jumper which is lying on top of a brick wall in Red Pitch and he puts it on. He rubs his body and does a light jog on the spot to keep warm. His gaze becomes fixed on a segment of the wall whilst he speaks.*

Remember this?

He points to dried blood on the wall of Red Pitch.

JOEY. Hard to forget. That was one scary fight.

BILAL. Everyone will remember that fight for as long as they live.

JOEY. As long as they live round endz, they'll forget it when they leave. (*Beat.*) That fight was epic! Did you see how long they were scrapping for?! Bare noise – so late, it was mad dark as well. Can you imagine if you'd missed it?!

BILAL. I know.

JOEY. Femz missed it – he said he didn't care though.

BILAL. Boy, I would've been gutted if I missed that fight.

JOEY. Bare blood was lost that day.

BILAL. Yeah... And it stayed on these brick walls.

Silence.

JOEY. I saw your dad the other day, you know. You know your dad doesn't speak loudly – he was like – (*Whispering.*) 'Hello Joseph, how are you?'

BILAL. Yeah, he told me.

JOEY (*whispering*). 'How's your mum? How's your dad? Say hello to them for me.'

BILAL. Allow it man. At least my dad isn't always shouting like your mum – wait… I think I can hear her now.

JOEY. Shut up bruv.

> BILAL *and* JOEY *laugh.*

> Do you think Femi's actually coming?

> BILAL *shrugs.*

> He ain't coming man. Omz is holding on.

BILAL. He always holds on.

> OMZ *re-enters with the ball and again ritualistically double-taps the cage. He puts the ball down and kicks it away.*

OMZ. Here.

> *He hands* BILAL *the tropical Sun Pride carton with half of the drink missing and gives him an opened Twix packet with only one bar left – it's clear he has eaten some of the Twix bar and has drunk half of the tropical juice.* BILAL*'s frustration goes undetected.*

> What did I miss? Esme was causing bare traffic, making bare noise.

JOEY. What?

OMZ. Yeah, talkin' 'bout 'YOU SHOULD BE ASHAMED, WE DON'T WANT A CHANGE.'

JOEY. Why?

OMZ. Who knows? She had signs and alla that – shouting on the roadside.

BILAL. Omz...

OMZ. Femi's still not here?! This guy is just unbelievable.

JOEY. I'm telling you man, let's just forget the two-on-two. Let's play *FIFA*.

BILAL. Omz...

OMZ. No man. We wait for Femz. We have to practise / for the trials.

BILAL. Omz!!

OMZ. Yo bro.

BILAL. What's this?

OMZ. Tropical juice... it says 'Sun Pride on it'... Oh 'and a Twix'.

OMZ *gives a cheeky smile and a wink.*

BILAL. Are you mad?! Go back.

OMZ. No, I will not go back. You asked for something and I delivered it.

BILAL *approaches* OMZ.

BILAL. You delivered half of it. Go back!

OMZ. Move.

JOEY *stands in between* OMZ *and* BILAL.

JOEY. If we go and play *FIFA*, we can go shop on the way.

BILAL. Go back!

OMZ. No chance.

JOEY. Chill you man.

BILAL. Go back bruv.

OMZ. I'm not going nowhere.

BILAL and OMZ *square up.* BILAL *headlocks* OMZ *and then they start play-fighting.* JOEY *shakes his head, disinterested.* OMZ *has the upper hand until…*

My hand – stop, my hand. You're biting now Bilz yeah?

They share a mischievous chuckle.

JOEY. You man, it's too dark to kick ball now and it's mad cold.

OMZ. Femi's such a let-down man. Man's moving to Kent tomorrow you know, where the bloodclart is Kent?

JOEY. Trust… that's dead.

Silence.

I'm telling you man, let's –

BILAL. First / on.

OMZ. First on. Me versus Bilz.

JOEY. By default, whoever's house it is, is first on. Whoever called 'first on' first, is also first on. So, it's me and Bilal on first.

The construction sounds rise in volume momentarily as more building equipment becomes distinct. We hear a singular voice chanting 'You should be ashamed, we don't want a change.' After a moment of this spike, it returns to normal and sustains.

Scene Two

BILAL *is onstage by himself with his football. It's pitch black around him but he is clearly visible. There are the occasional flashes of light implying a photographer is taking pictures. We hear the sound of a picture being taken each time we see a flash. We also hear a roaring crowd. It should feel like the commercials that usually emerge around the time of World Cup competitions – stadium-esque. BILAL is pretending to be a football commentator as he does what he says.*

BILAL. '"Drop, drop" shoulder to one, "drop, drop" shoulder to two... no, no, I don't believe it, "drop, drop" shoulder three times. Bilal is through on goal; Bilal shoots, he scores and the crowd goes wild!! I swear you'll never see anything like this again!!!'

BILAL *celebrates his goal. More flashing lights, and louder roars from the crowd.*

OMZ. 'Crowd goes wild', yeah?

OMZ *appears at the gate of Red Pitch, taking us out of this state and back to normal. He double-taps the cage upon entry.*

BILAL (*whilst 'drop, drop' shouldering*). Come on. Them 'drop, drop' shoulders are serious!

OMZ *spots BILAL's rucksack in the corner of Red Pitch.*

OMZ. You didn't take your bag to your yard?

BILAL. Na man, time wasted. I'm trying to get my work in.

OMZ *pauses.*

OMZ. Bro, you live just there.

BILAL *continues practising.*

Where's Joey?

BILAL *shoots OMZ a look and then dribbles with the football.*

BILAL. You know where Joey is.

OMZ. Relaxxx. Don't you know how to rest?

BILAL. Listen, let me educate you: anything you want in life, you're gonna have to work twice as hard to get it.

OMZ takes the ball.

OMZ. I don't work hard, I work smart. You have to rest as well or you're gonna burn out. We've just come from a match.

BILAL. Yeah, but it was a friendly. When we make it pro, we'll be playing up to three times a week, you know.

BILAL takes the ball back.

OMZ. Yeah, I know.

BILAL. Things are gonna have to change when we go clear bruv, I'm telling you. I saw some post on Insta saying that ballers even switch up the food they eat as well.

OMZ. Not me boy. I'll be having my curry goat and rice for breakfast, rice 'n' peas with stew chicken for lunch and tuwo shinkafa and miyan taushe for dinner and still be badding it up on the pitch. (*Referencing the ball.*) Yeah.

BILAL. What do you know about tuwo shinkafa and miyan taushe?

BILAL passes the ball to OMZ.

OMZ. That time your mum made some for me, Rara and my grandad init.

BILAL. Oh yeahhh. You can come back whenever you know – my mum was gassed having you lot around.

OMZ is grateful but struggles to show it. He passes the ball back to BILAL.

OMZ. Coach needs to hurry up and send us them deets for trials.

BILAL. He said he'll text us tonight.

OMZ. He better or I'll slap his head bruv.

BILAL. Do it.

OMZ. Coach thinks he's hard but he ain't about it.

BILAL. He grew up in endz you know.

OMZ. So? He dipped time ago.

BILAL. Only 'cause his flat had mice.

OMZ. Didn't you hear Coach talking crud today? Talking 'bout, how he don't wanna ever see me holding the ball for too long. My guy, if I feel like dribbling pass the whole team and scoring, I'll do it.

BILAL. Na, you don't have it in your locker.

OMZ. Look at how you're hating.

BILAL (*extends his arms and hands*). Why would I hate?

OMZ (*mockingly, whilst extending arms and hands*). 'Why would I hate?' That's how I know you're capping.

BILAL. There's nothing to hate on. Coach always says I remind him of a young Sancho.

OMZ. Sancho's not that sick.

BILAL. Now you're capping. On form, he's one of the hardest in the league – Coach says it all the time.

OMZ. Yeah, only 'cause he used to train him up when they lived local.

BILAL. Whatever man. Imagine, Sancho came from endz and he's playing pro.

OMZ. We up next, InshāAllah.

BILAL. InshāAllah, most definitely.

OMZ. I used to see Sanch on the blocks, he used to come Red Pitch.

BILAL. 'Sanch' you know? He doesn't know you bro.

OMZ. Jadon Sancho came Red Pitch once you wasteman and I saw him when I was coming back from mosque. He nodded at me.

BILAL (*hysterical laughter*). He don't knooow youuuuu!!

OMZ. It's mad how you're an Omz hater in disguise.

BILAL. 'Omz hater'? What do I hate on?

OMZ. You hate on me 'cause I'm a better baller.

BILAL. Better what?!

OMZ. That's why I was top goal-scorer today.

BILAL. Bro, let it go. You scored one / more goal than me.

OMZ. I scored more 'cause I'm a better footballer. Brudda, look at the goals I was scoring last season. Thirty-yarders, you could never.

BILAL. I bagged most goals last season. In the whole Sunday league.

OMZ. Ah, 'last season', 'last season', 'last season'; is that all you know?

BILAL. *You* brought it up!

OMZ. If Coach let me take free kicks and pens, I would have netted more than you. I was second highest.

BILAL. I was top assists as well, you were nowhere near.

OMZ. No one cares about assists. It's about goals. Goals win you games.

BILAL. Bro, we'll just ask Joey who's better.

OMZ. We all know who your biggest fan is gonna select.

BILAL. Cap. About 'biggest fan'. (*Beat.*) Where is this guy, anyway? He's taking his time.

OMZ. Alie? All he knows is fast food after matches.

BILAL. Don't act like you're not gonna ask him for some.

OMZ (*smiling mischievously*). I might, still.

BILAL *shakes his head; he lets out a chuckle*.

Remember back in the day, when we were playing runouts with the olders and Joey – this guy – he was getting shook of tagging the olders, so we always lost. They'd be like 'Na, don't touch me. I don't care, don't touch me.' And he was like 'It's the game though' but he'd never touch them. Paigon...

BILAL *chuckles and shakes his head.*

He knows a lot of things but he's not street-smart. (*Beat.*) We need to make sure we do a farewell match for him before he goes.

BILAL. When does Joey move?

OMZ. I don't even know. His new crib's got a proper garden though – he's gassed.

BILAL. He has all that garden space to work on his tekkers.

OMZ. 'Tekkers'? Joey's already said he's gonna be having bare summer barbecues. Bringing through bare gyal.

BILAL. He's not serious – (*Beat.*) Na, runouts was a motive, back in the day.

OMZ. What? I'm always gonna be down for runouts.

BILAL. So, you're gonna be a big man playing runouts, yeah? Basically, playing tag around endz like a jobless human. Leave that for the youngers.

OMZ. Brudda, you're never too old for them tings. (*Beat.*) I'm even gonna be banging out Red Pitch with my youts. Gonna say: 'Now listen children, this was where Papa scored the greatest goal Red Pitch had ever seen... and this was where Papa weightsed Uncle Bilal off the ball and sent him to the gym.'

BILAL. You're gonna lie to your kids like that...

They share a chuckle.

How many kids you having?

OMZ. Seven, one for every day of the week.

BILAL *thinks for a moment.*

BILAL. I rate it still.

He nudges OMZ.

OMZ. What 'bout you?

BILAL. I'm gonna have twins. Boy and girl – I'm gonna be
doing up project Mbappe with both of them. On them daily –
no time-wasting. 'Drop, drop' shoulder... easy.

OMZ *shakes his head.*

I can't believe you said you're better than me, man. The
nerve. My left toe is better than your whole right leg.

OMZ *(laughing).* Wasteman.

BILAL. What do you have better than me?

OMZ. Everything.

BILAL. Like what?

OMZ. I'm faster than you.

BILAL. Paddiiiinnn.

OMZ. I don't know why you're making all this noise brudda.

BILAL. Aight, cool, know what...

BILAL *goes to one end of Red Pitch, assuming the starting
position taken up in 100m sprints.*

OMZ. Get up man! I don't wanna embarrass you.

BILAL. Quick race, there and back.

OMZ. Brudda, I keep telling you man: this is Omz! You lot
need to respeck it. Are you forgetting what I did when we
wiped Eastside Rovers last season? When I gapped their
number eight? You know donny was mad fast as well. Ahh
na, the way I'll put you in a spliff and smoke you Bilz...

BILAL. Let's just race and see init.

OMZ *thinks for a second. It looks like he's walking over to
join* BILAL *on the start line... but he goes to get the football.*

OMZ. Like I said, I ain't tryna burn out. I worked hard today.
When I'm more rested init.

BILAL. Shook yout. Pass.

OMZ. Why would I be 'shook'? I'm the fastest in the whole estate.

BILAL. Pshhh, maybe when I move out – (*Beat.*) Pass.

OMZ (*startled, ignoring* BILAL*'s request*). What? When you moving?

BILAL. Pass the ball!

OMZ *feigns to pass the ball to* BILAL, *chuckling whilst doing so.*

Aight cool...

BILAL *approaches* OMZ *with purpose.* OMZ *can't help but giggle. He serendipitously gets the ball through* BILAL*'s legs.* OMZ*'s laughter grows in response to the nutmeg.*

OMZ. Ay! Red Pitch rules, if it goes through your legs, that's two bangs.

BILAL. Don't touch me bruv.

JOEY *enters, ritualistically double-tapping the cage. He has a chicken-and-chip-shop box in his hands.*

You took your time.

OMZ. For real, it was getting a little late – thought you got that 'home-time' call.

JOEY (*dismissing* OMZ). Bruv, you know the Morley's on Wooly Road has closed? Guess what's there now... A Costa. I go in, I'm like, 'Rah there ain't no wings here, what happened to Morley's?' They're all like 'What?' I said 'Morley's, where's the chicken-and-chip shop?' He goes... 'It's not here any more,' I'm like 'I can see that, where am I meant to get my barbecue wings and chips from?' He tells me they sell soup... Soup bruv. I know I don't go Wooly Road a lot but when did that Morley's change?!

BILAL. You went HFC then?

JOEY. You're smoking. Only Morley's give you that good chicken – I walked down to Camberwell. That's why I took long.

BILAL *shakes his head and goes to practise shooting.*
JOEY *starts eating. As he eats, he notices* OMZ *ogling his food.* OMZ *walks over to* JOEY. JOEY *rolls his eyes.*

OMZ. What you saying though? What you saying?

JOEY. Yeah, I'm good… you?

OMZ. What you saying? What did you get?

JOEY (*apathetically*). Four wings and chips.

OMZ. Four wings and chips, yeah?! Did you get burger sauce?

JOEY. No.

OMZ. You didn't get burger sauce?

JOEY. No.

OMZ. Fair enough, fair enough – (*Beat.*) You put salt on it though?

JOEY *rolls his eyes.*

BILAL. Bro, just leave him to enjoy his food.

OMZ. Why you getting involved for Bilal? (*Beat.*) So what, you put salt on it?

JOEY. Do you want some chips?

OMZ. If you're offering.

OMZ *takes a wing from* JOEY*'s chicken-and-chips box.*

JOEY. Oi, what you doing? Yo, put it back.

OMZ *licks the wing.*

OMZ. You sure?

OMZ *walks off eating the chicken wing. When it's done, he puts the bone in the chicken-and-chip-shop bag which* JOEY *has left on the side.*

JOEY. You owe me a wing.

OMZ. Yeah, I'll pattern that.

JOEY *kisses his teeth and shakes his head.*

JOEY. The way they're changing endz is nuts.

OMZ. They're not changing it. They're renewing it.

JOEY. They're taking everything good.

OMZ. 'They're taking everything good'? Listen to this conspiracy theorist, again.

JOEY. It's not a conspiracy bro. Am I lying Bilz?

BILAL. Boy… I ain't deeped it too much to be honest.

JOEY. You need to watch what's happening. Everything on endz is changing. It's a madness.

OMZ. Can you imagine? They're patterning endz and you're moving like you don't want them to do it. Look at it. It's a shambles – rotting everywhere, it stinks, lifts don't work.

JOEY. Obviously, I want them to fix it up but not if they're gonna take all the sick spots away. All the people as well. Femz has gone. I'm going Monday. Bilz is gonna go. Even you're gonna have to go.

OMZ. No I'm not. I'm staying on endz. My block of flats are the last to go down on Reedbury. We're just gonna move into the new ones.

BILAL. You're gonna be the only one on endz? That's dead.

OMZ. Na, it's gonna be lit, deep it. I'll just be banging out Red Pitch and going back to my brand-new crib literally thirty seconds away. It's gonna be a ground-floor ting as well so my grandad won't have to walk up to the fifth floor. And anyways the lifts are gonna be working so it don't matter. It's gonna be sick!

BILAL *and* JOEY *don't truly agree with what* OMZ *has said. They avoid eye contact with him, exchanging glances with each other.* OMZ *notices.*

Just 'cause you have to go Camberwell to get chicken and chips don't mean them renewing endz is a bad thing.

OMZ forces a laugh but BILAL *and* JOEY *don't laugh with him. They pass between one another.*

BILAL (*to* JOEY). Who's a better baller, me or Omz?

JOEY *ponders.*

JOEY. It's me obviously.

BILAL. Forget it.

JOEY. 'Cause I'm a goalie, I can't be the best?

BILAL. No one said that – But yes – Aight, who's faster?

JOEY *thinks.*

JOEY. I don't know. Just race init.

BILAL. He's shook.

OMZ. Low all that 'bout 'shook'.

JOEY. Race then. (*Beat.*) To be fair, I'll probably take both you man in a race.

OMZ. What?!

BILAL. My ears!

OMZ. Come! Joey can never be disrespecting like that.

OMZ goes to one end of Red Pitch, assuming the starting position taken up in 100m sprints.

JOEY. Come then.

JOEY *joins in the starting position.*

BILAL. Come we go. There and back yeah?

Then BILAL. *They are all on the line.*

OMZ. Calm.

Beat – OMZ *tries to creep forward.*

Ay no cheating you man. No cheating, yeah? Ay? Bilz. No cheating.

JOEY. Can you get back on the line?

OMZ (*mischievously*). Oh my mistake. (*Beat*.) Are we gonna go on 'go' or 'on your marks'?

BILAL stands from his starting position, frustrated.

BILAL. When do you ever go on, 'on your marks'?

OMZ. Cool, cool. Come.

OMZ gets into his start position, as does BILAL.

BILAL. Cool. On, your marks...

OMZ. Get set, go!

OMZ bursts out the blocks.

BILAL. Cheat!

BILAL follows desperately trying to catch OMZ. JOEY's phone rings, distracting him from the race. He takes it out to see who's calling. OMZ wins the race, much to BILAL's annoyance.

You're a cheat. You cheater. Rematch!

OMZ celebrates and then notices JOEY's phone which is still ringing.

OMZ. 'Oh boyyyyy – home time.'

He shows it to BILAL and OMZ.

JOEY. It's Coach.

BILAL. Bro, answer it!

He answers. BILAL and OMZ crowd around JOEY.

JOEY. Coach! Good. Yeah, I'm with them now. Alright. Na... cool... I'll tell them... cool, alright, thanks, bye.

JOEY locks off and says nothing for a moment. BILAL and OMZ stare eagerly at him.

Sunday 3rd August. Blaisewall Park. Get there for 10:30 a.m. QPR trials!

They jump excitedly in a huddle together.

ALL. Ayyy!!!!

OMZ stops.

OMZ. Wait, I'm linking a girl at 10:30 a.m. on Sunday 3rd August.

They all stop jumping.

BILAL *and* JOEY. Shut up man!

OMZ jumps excitedly again.

OMZ. Ayyyyy!

BILAL *and* JOEY *jump excitedly in a huddle together again with* OMZ.

ALL. Ayyyyy!

BILAL. From now on lads, no messing around. We put in this work. No lacking!

The construction sounds rise in volume momentarily. After a moment of this spike, the construction returns to normal and sustains.

Scene Three

BILAL, JOEY *and* OMZ *are in Red Pitch doing warm-up exercises without the ball. It feels intense. Suddenly and seamlessly,* BILAL, JOEY *and* OMZ *have moved on to ball work. They are passing and moving; it's rapid, it's focused, it's choreographed between them. Another change as* JOEY *is now in goal.* BILAL *and* OMZ *are shooting at him. Finally, their practising comes to an end as the football has gone into the scaffoldings.*

BILAL. Yeah, go on Joey.

JOEY. What?

BILAL. Get my ball init.

JOEY. Wait, why me? It's Omz that should be getting it.

OMZ. Is it my fault it's in the scaffoldings?

JOEY. You're the one that kicked it there.

OMZ. I shot and you fingertipped it over.

JOEY. Ahh! Bilal if I *fingertip* it over, alie it's already going out the pitch?

OMZ. Don't matter Joey.

JOEY. Yes, it does 'cause whether I touched it or not, it was already going out.

OMZ. The rule is: it's whoever touches it last, gets it.

JOEY. Na man, that's like saying: someone dashes an Audemars Piguet from the eighth floor and I fingertip it when it's coming down… am I the one that broke it?

BILAL (*considering it*). I hear you, I hear you.

OMZ. What are you talking about? It's like saying: I shoot, keeper fingertips it over and it's a corner for me… 'cause you touched it last.

JOEY. No – (*Realising.*) Wait?

OMZ (*assuming victory*). There you go.

BILAL (*flatteringly*). You got them watches secured to be dashing them, yeah Joey?

BILAL *spuds* JOEY.

JOEY. Soon come, soon come.

BILAL (*flatteringly*). Yeahhh? (*Suddenly serious.*) But get my ball.

OMZ. Joey, why do you always have to make things so difficult?

BILAL *and* JOEY *are startled.*

JOEY. Ahhh! Me?!

BILAL (*shocked*). You have the temerity to say someone else makes things difficult? Mr I'm-Not-Going-Anywhere. Mr-I-Want-to-Fight-Everybody. Wow.

JOEY. Thank you!

OMZ*'s phone vibrates. He continues speaking whilst taking it out of his pocket.*

OMZ. Joey, I know what you're doing.

JOEY. What?

OMZ. You think you're sick.

OMZ *answers his phone.* BILAL *and* JOEY *wait.*

(*On the phone.*) Rara, you okay? I left some rice 'n' peas in the fridge for you...

BILAL (*to the phone*). Rahim, tell your brother someone needs to be getting my ball. (*Beat.*) We miss you bro, come Red Pitch.

OMZ *walks away from* BILAL *and* JOEY. *They're watching him.*

OMZ. What?! I told him before I left – 'Don't turn it off from the main switch 'cause you'll break the boiler!' This donny doesn't listen. Did you switch it back on for him? What's he doing now? Alright, keep an eye on him. Cool. You good? Calm. Cool, shout me if you need me. Love you. Love.

OMZ *hangs up. He pockets his phone and, slightly irritated, rejoins* BILAL *and* JOEY. JOEY *quickly moves the conversation forward.*

JOEY. I've actually been thinking you man, you know what we should do? Vlog when we're in Red Pitch, then just @ bare professional teams to scout us from that.

OMZ. That's not a bad idea you know... 'Hey everybody, welcome to our channel.'

OMZ *does a sudden sprint on the spot.*

'Look at the strength… look at the strength!'

JOEY. Trust, it could bang you know. You gotta shoot your shot.

BILAL. We're gonna blow on Sunday so we don't need to do no vlog.

JOEY. Yeah God-willing but say we *don't*?

BILAL. We're gonna blow, Joey.

JOEY. Trust me, you always need a back-up plan. Like me, I'm gonna do Business Law on the side. Omz, you're doing Art and Design, you're sick at that stuff, you could be the next… painter guy init, and Bilz, you're doing Maths, you could be a banker.

BILAL. Bro, you shouldn't think like that. If you think about not making it, then you won't. It's a mindset thing.

JOEY. I knowww but it's always good to have a plan B. I've been paying attention to this whole 'buying a house' set-up. It's biiig money.

OMZ. I ain't seeking the dunyā, my brudda. So long as my grandad and Rara are good.

BILAL. For real, the goal's not to make money, it's to be successful.

JOEY *kisses his teeth.*

JOEY. Can you be successful without money? You think you can just walk into the shop and ask for an Audemars without the P? Listen, when you're doing your thing in the bank, Omz – you're painting your art, I'm doing law – we can come back to endz, buy flats together, then sell them for like fifty thousand each. Minimum. Trust me – we'll be securing that Urus ASAP!

JOEY *recites rap lyrics celebrating Lamborghinis. He looks at* BILAL *to finish the lyrics but, instead of picking up the cue,* BILAL *stares blankly at* JOEY. JOEY *finishes the rap himself, reciting the next line.*

BILAL. The way you're moving, it's like you're not even on ball.

JOEY. Obviously I'm on ball. I'm just saying it's good to have options.

OMZ. Rah boy. Fifty bags for a flat on endz?

BILAL. Don't listen to this guy. That ain't true. Even I know it's four hundred bags minimum.

OMZ. What?!

JOEY. How do you know?

BILAL. My mum and dad went to one of them local meetings.

OMZ. Ay, when you moving Bilal?

BILAL. I don't know yet. I still need to pattern some things...

OMZ. But you're definitely moving?

JOEY. He has to.

OMZ. No, he doesn't.

JOEY. His flats are going down next.

OMZ. So?

JOEY *shakes his head.*

Pause.

JOEY. I'm just saying if anyone should be making Ps off endz, it's us.

OMZ. 'Making Ps off endz'? If anything, you're supposed to be giving Ps back to endz.

JOEY. Giving back? This is why I'm predicted a seven in business and you're predicted a six.

OMZ. Whatever man, if people gave back to Reedbury in the first place, then they wouldn't be renewing it. But nobody put P back in the endz, nobody took care of it, so it's getting patterned now.

JOEY. It's not the people that need to be putting P back in endz. Do you know how much money the government and all them organisations have? Trust me. I heard my mum talking about it.

BILAL. I heard your mum talking about that as well actually... in fact, if you listen closely...

JOEY. You're both not serious guys.

BILAL *laughs*.

OMZ. Come we play pounds.

JOEY (*excitedly*). Come!

JOEY *and* OMZ *take out pound coins each and stand in front of a wall in Red Pitch. As they are setting up to play 'pounds' (penny up the wall), they are interrupted by* BILAL.

BILAL. Hello, na, na, na – one of you man need to be climbing right now.

OMZ. Jump in Bilz, it'll be like the old days.

BILAL. We're not trying to make it like the 'old days'. We need to focus on *today* so the new days will be patterned.

OMZ (*dismissively*). Ah yeah, cool story bro.

BILAL *stands in front of the wall that* JOEY *and* OMZ *are playing pounds at, obstructing the game.*

Ay Bilz, move man! We're trying to do something here.

BILAL. Are you mad? And my football's still in the scaffolding.

JOEY. Bro, *you* get it if you want it so much then – move man!!

OMZ. Whaaattt?! Joseph?!!... Is this how you're talking to Bilal now yeahhh? Joey from the blocks, yeahhh? I rate it. Spud me.

OMZ *forces a nudge from* JOEY.

BILAL. Joey, don't try it 'cause I'll just wipe you.

OMZ (*stirring*). 'Wipe you.' 'WIPE YOU', you know. Personally, I wouldn't have it.

JOEY (*to* OMZ). Be quiet / man.

OMZ (*reprimanding*). Na, na, don't be stepping to me like that, I'm not Bilz – you'll get spun straight away.

JOEY *kisses his teeth.*

JOEY (*holding his pound coin*). Come.

BILAL. No man – my ball. You man, listen. Trials ain't too far away. This is a one-time opportunity. One-time, do you get it? We need to put in that work from now, we need to be ready. The competition to get in is gonna be nuts – other man from other teams are gonna be there, grown men – proper ringed-out uncles with families saying that they're sixteen years old – they're gonna be there. So we have to be ready. We need the ball. We need to practise.

JOEY. Bilz, we've been practising for time.

BILAL. 'Success comes after tears.'

BILAL *focuses on* JOEY.

Joey, you *did* touch it last. And that's like the oldest Red Pitch rule.

JOEY *sighs.*

Imagine the earnings we'll be making when we get in…

JOEY *thinks. After a moment, he shakes his head.*

JOEY. You think you're sick, you know.

BILAL. Lambos, Rolls-Royces, Ranges… we'd have all of that.

JOEY *is pondering.* BILAL *watches on.*

JOEY *shakes his head. He starts to walk out.*

Thank you Joey. Thank you. Thank you, for being mature.

JOEY. Come, help me though.

BILAL *shoots* OMZ *a mischievous grin as he walks out of Red Pitch with* JOEY. *They exit, ritualistically double-tapping the cage, leaving* OMZ *in Red Pitch alone. He looks around the space. He walks around for a moment, taking it all in. He browses his phone briefly before putting it away.*

*He then imagines himself as a professional footballer –
a moment still grounded in the real world. He commentates on
what he does as he does it with an imaginary ball – it's
understated.*

OMZ (*imitating a commentator*). Omar Richards is through on
goal, he shoots and scores on his debut!

*OMZ blows two kisses to the crowd. He begins to pray,
stood with open palms facing upwards and his eyes closed –
a tranquil moment. JOEY enters, ritualistically double-
tapping the cage and startling OMZ.*

JOEY. Ay yo, guess what?

OMZ. Wagwarn?

JOEY. Ah actually, I'll wait till Bilz comes back.

OMZ. Where is he?

JOEY. With his dad.

OMZ. Getting a lecture…?

JOEY. Boy. (*Beat.*) When he comes back, I bet you I could get
Bilal to say: 'Why do I care?' Arms out like this.
(*Demonstrates.*) You know when he's doing that, he's
capping. He definitely cares.

OMZ (*chuckling*). Word. How you gonna do that?

JOEY. You'll see. I got some tea. My Snap is popping off.

OMZ (*sternly*). Tell me.

JOEY. You'll see.

OMZ. Tell me before I twist your ear.

JOEY. You man can't bully me any more you know. I'm a big
boy now.

OMZ squares up to JOEY.

Okay, okay okay.

Beat.

Jameela's having a party.

OMZ. Say swear! Yeah, he's definitely doing, 'why do I care', arms out. Ha!

JOEY. Trust me. You gonna come?

OMZ. Maybe, maybe.

JOEY. Lola from St Bernadette's is gonna be there.

OMZ. Lola from St Bernadette's?!

JOEY *nods*.

That girl has the fattest Bundesliga! Mi deyah.

JOEY. Trust, it's gonna be litty. (*Beat*.) You still on pounds? I'm lardy.

OMZ. Come then.

OMZ *throws his coin. It lands far away from the wall.* JOEY *throws his coin which lands closer.*

JOEY. Jheeze!

JOEY *walks over to collect the coins.* JOEY *flips the coins. He calls it whilst the coins are in the air.*

Heads.

The coins land on the ground. OMZ *has a look and then hastily swipes his coin and backs away, laughing mischievously.* JOEY *picks up his coin and shakes his head.*

You are the sorest loser.

OMZ. You don't even need the P.

JOEY. Says who?

OMZ. Brudda, you got a Gucci belt. Your family are rich.

JOEY. We're not rich, we're doing alright.

OMZ. Just 'alright' ya kna? Rematch, come.

JOEY. If you cheat again...

OMZ. Yeah, yeah, yeah.

They get in position to throw their coins but are halted by their conversation.

What's Bilal's dad saying to him?

JOEY *shrugs.*

JOEY. He should keep him there man. Before he comes back talking 'bout practising. This guy doesn't know how to chill.

OMZ. You know why he's like that though, init?

JOEY *and* OMZ *look at each other.*

Remember when Bilz missed that sitter last season and his dad didn't even look at him once when he was driving us home.

JOEY. For real. It's mad 'cause he's usually safe.

OMZ. Yeah, he is, *usually.* He gives me and Rara money any time he sees us. He was proper tight with my grandad as well. They used to go mosque but –

JOEY. How is your grandad anyway?

OMZ. He's calm. He's just getting older init. But he's calm.

JOEY. If you need my mum to fast-track appointments at hospital again, that's no wahalas at all.

OMZ *is grateful but struggles to show it.*

OMZ. These dead scaffoldings. Bruv, I don't know who asked for them.

JOEY. If there ain't no scaffoldings, they ain't ever gonna be able to build your new crib.

OMZ. Obviously, I know that.

Beat.

JOEY. I don't get it; how can you see all the people cutting from endz but think them changing it is good?

OMZ *shakes his head.*

OMZ. No one can tell me them renewing endz ain't gonna be lit for my grandad.

JOEY. But bro, that's like saying –

OMZ. Just let it go Joey. Why do you want me to be wrong so bad? You think you know everything; you don't, my guy. Let it go.

JOEY. Alright, cool – pounds. Come.

BILAL *returns, double-tapping the cage upon entry, interrupting the idea of a rematch – he has his ball.*

BILAL. Joey, you lodge.

JOEY. What took you so long, anyway? You were struggling to hear your dad, init?

BILAL (*sarcastically*). Hahaha. Your mum doesn't do long-distance phone calls, she just shouts. (*Beat.*) Ay let's get to work, man! My dad was saying that stamina is one of the main things scouts look for – let's keep going!

JOEY *signals to* OMZ *that he's going to provoke the desired reaction from* BILAL *imminently,*

JOEY. Ay Bilz, Jameela's having a party, you know.

BILAL. Cool. I'm not going.

JOEY. It's gonna be local.

BILAL. Don't talk to me 'bout that girl!

JOEY. I'm gonna go.

BILAL. Enjoy.

JOEY. You coming as well?

BILAL. Nope you'll be on your ones. I know Omz ain't gonna go.

JOEY *is a little confused* BILAL *hasn't reacted in the predicted way.* OMZ *signals to* JOEY, *he'll get him to react – 'Why do I care?' – with his arms out.*

OMZ. I'm going.

BILAL. What you gonna do there?

OMZ. Gonna grab some wines.

BILAL. Who?

OMZ. Me fam.

BILAL. Which wines? The drinking wines?

OMZ. Deadest banter. Brudda, sometimes yeah... it's like... have a little fun, my guy.

JOEY. You gotta let it go Bilz.

BILAL. Bro, let's not talk about her. She's a distraction.

JOEY. How?

BILAL. Are we not meant to be kicking ball right now? There you go. She's distracting us.

OMZ. It flopped Joey. He ain't doing it.

BILAL. Doing what?

JOEY (*to* OMZ). Yeah it did. Ah well. (*To* BILAL.) Come though, man. I get Jameela's your ex but bro... she personally told me to invite you.

BILAL. Say swear?

JOEY. I could show you on Snap.

> JOEY *gets out his phone and shows* BILAL. BILAL *walks away, licks his lips and smiles – he's gassed.*

See my guy! It's gonna be local as well. It's in the hall on endz.

OMZ. Ain't that closed?

JOEY. It's closing. That's how she got it so cheap.

BILAL. When is it?

JOEY. Friday.

BILAL. Two days before trials? Forget that man.

JOEY. Just deep it Bilz, if you come and wine with next gyal, even collect couple socials, then she's gonna be mad for leaving you for Zack.

BILAL. I was gonna leave her anyway.

JOEY *and* OMZ *glance at each other, holding in a laugh.*

OMZ. Be real bro.

BILAL. I am being real.

JOEY. You were slyly gutted when she left you.

BILAL. No, I weren't.

JOEY. It hurt you *and* she left you for Zack... Zack?!

BILAL (*arms out*). Why do I care?

JOEY *and* OMZ *look at each other and then burst out laughing. They celebrate this moment.*

What?

JOEY. We know you're capping bro.

OMZ *imitates the arms out to* BILAL.

BILAL (*ignoring them*). But real talk, of all the people to go out with...

OMZ. It's cool, he probably tried to take Jameela from you to get back at us from when we wiped him in primary school.

JOEY. Ohhh yeahh, the way you man did him was dirty. Omz came sprinting from nowhere to back it, I was surprised.

OMZ (*laughing*). He didn't want it!

They all laugh.

Joey, your farewell match? We should do it now.

JOEY. There's only three of us so we can't do two-on-two. It's gotta be FA. On Wednesday, after training?

OMZ. Calm.

BILAL. Calm.

The construction sounds rise in volume. At the same time, the 'You should be ashamed, we don't want a change' chants are heard and are coming from a group now. After a moment of this spike, the chants fade out and the construction returns to normal and sustains.

Scene Four

OMZ *is in Red Pitch alone. He is visibly agitated whilst he does exercises without the ball (explosive sprints, high-knees, sidesteps). He rests. After a moment, he returns to doing exercises. Finally,* BILAL *and* JOEY *arrive with their rucksacks on and with* BILAL's *ball. They ritualistically double-tap the cage upon entry.*

BILAL. Wagwarn.

OMZ. You man got here quick. Pass.

BILAL. Bro, what happened?

OMZ *kisses his teeth.*

OMZ. What do you mean what happened?

BILAL. Are you gonna apologise to Coach?

OMZ. Apologise? For what?

BILAL. Bro, you violated.

JOEY. You sent for him differently.

OMZ. He sent for me. How can he be making me run laps for that long? Is he mad?

JOEY. He does it all the time. If you're late to training, he makes you run laps.

OMZ. For that long?

JOEY. But you were an hour late though.

OMZ. Fifty minutes.

JOEY. Bro. Listen, if you want, you can just use my phone to dial –

OMZ. I ain't calling him, Joey. He should apologise to me.

JOEY. Coach said he's taking your name off the list for trials.

OMZ. Why?

BILAL. What do you mean 'why'? You stormed out of training. And it looked like you were 'bout to scrap him.

OMZ. He was stepping in my face init. (*Beat.*) I don't even care.

BILAL. Why you capping for, Omz? It's QPR trials. That's a sick team. You can bad that up, put in that transfer request to Arsenal, then be killing it there. (*Trying to force a laugh out of* OMZ.) Obviously, I'll be 'drop, drop' shouldering at Man United, so we'll be collecting all the trophies but you can still be a club legend.

JOEY (*also trying to force a laugh out of* OMZ). Na, na, it'll be Chelsea winning that silverware bro. Me with them golden gloves.

BILAL. Let's not talk about teams that buy leagues. See what I'm saying though, Omz? Imagine… All of us… for our teams… that's gonna be lit.

OMZ. Yo, Joey's farewell match. Come we play.

BILAL. Bro, you're gonna throw it away over something petty? We could be securing that bag as well.

JOEY. That's true. You don't even have a plan B. That's why I was saying we should buy houses –

OMZ. Don't start all that Joey.

JOEY. Bro, I don't want you to be broke.

BILAL. Yeah, he won't be 'cause he's gonna be a baller.

OMZ. You're telling me what I'm gonna do with my own life? Come out of here man. Are we doing your match or not?

BILAL. I'm not telling you what to do with your life. I'm just saying ball is what we're *meant* to do. Together. Do you get it? How long have we been waiting for a chance like this to come up? Now we have it, don't throw it away over something petty.

OMZ. Fam, you lot are getting on my nerves.

BILAL. Doesn't the Prophet speak about forgiveness?

JOEY. The Bible says, don't let the sun go down on your wrath.

Pause.

OMZ. How did you lot get back so quick?

BILAL. Omz –

JOEY (*interrupting*). Sandra.

OMZ. Reedbury Sandra?

JOEY. She saw us at the bus stop, pulled up on us, and was like – (*Cockney accent.*) 'Get in.' 'Blimey!' That's all she kept saying, 'Blimey, look at how big you boys have gotten. Blimey.'

BILAL. Sandra's calm man.

JOEY. Oh yeah, she said to round up the lads from the area too, they're trying to close down Esme's dry cleaner's, Sandy's coming back to protest and she's saying we should come through.

BILAL. Listen man, I'll tell Coach you said sorry.

OMZ. Don't get involved.

BILAL. My dad's even trying to become an agent. He could sort out contracts for us. Everything is patterned Omz.

OMZ. For him to pressure me? I'm good.

BILAL. Pressure?

Beat.

OMZ. Joey, go in goal.

BILAL. Omz, I'm thinking 'bout the long term. 'Success comes after tears', remember? You have to make it or else all this work you've been putting in… it counts for nothing. Absolutely nothing. And there's so many people counting on you as well. You've got Rahim, your grandad.

JOEY. It's true, and then if you don't come, you *have* to start thinking 'bout what you're doing after college, like what uni you're going to. Can't just expect things to be calm. You have to do the resear–

BILAL. He's going to trials and he's getting in, Joey – Just 'llow all that. (*To* OMZ.) Fix up bruv, what's wrong with you? Stop being petty.

OMZ. I'm not being petty! My grandad fell down in our block coming back from the GP… it's not easy climbing to the fifth floor when you're eighty-one. That's why I was late yeah!

A moment, BILAL and JOEY do not know what to say. OMZ storms out, but still ritualistically double-tapping the cage.

JOEY. I feel bad, still.

BILAL sighs.

I asked him, he said his grandad was cool, just getting older. Coach would 'llow him if he tells him.

BILAL sighs and shrugs.

He should've just shouted my mum for help. She could've taken his grandad GP.

BILAL. You know Omz is stubborn.

JOEY. There's that but also… he's probably getting used to doing things one man up.

Pause.

BILAL. It's Omz bro. He'll be fine.

The construction sounds rise in volume momentarily and then return to normal.

JOEY. Have your parents found a new spot yet?

BILAL *shrugs.*

Bro, you need to pay attention to what's going on. All you know is football.

BILAL. Ah leave it Joey. We got trials on Sunday, obviously football is the focus.

JOEY. Yeah, but if you don't find a spot, they'll just move you out into the / sticks.

BILAL. I don't care about all that. When I get in at trials, my money will take care of everything.

JOEY. So you do wanna be rich then?

BILAL. I wanna be successful, like I said.

JOEY. I'm just saying you have to get on that bro, or at least get your parents to get on / that.

BILAL. I have! I am. There's this online thing you have to do. My parents don't know what they're doing so I'm looking into it.

JOEY. What do you mean 'looking into it'? Get professional support if your parents are struggling. You have to go to the right people to help you from early or you're gonna get left / behind.

BILAL. Just leave it Joey!!... Leave it.

Silence. BILAL goes off to do some ball work whilst JOEY goes on his phone, browsing. After a moment BILAL takes in his surroundings. He gets out his phone and starts taking pictures of the pitch, the rusting goals, the hole in the AstroTurf, blood on the wall. JOEY notices.

JOEY. You good? You're moving like a tourist.

BILAL. It's for when I go init. (*Beat.*) I wonder if them olders look back on this fight and laugh about it...

JOEY. Probably not, the way they scrapped was too dirty. Probably don't even speak.

BILAL. For real.

The construction sounds rise in volume. After a moment, the construction returns to normal and sustains.

Scene Five

BILAL, JOEY *and* OMZ *are in Red Pitch. They're not dressed in their football clothes – instead, they are dressed dressy casual having just come from Jameela's birthday party. There is no ball, it's just vibes.* JOEY *has a plastic cup sipping what appears at first to be… alcohol? He's in a good mood, dancing, rapping and singing.* BILAL *is laughing, also in a good mood.* OMZ *is keeping it casual but he's quite happy too.*

BILAL. You're yakked fam.

JOEY (*pushing the plastic cup towards* BILAL). Come, drink some.

BILAL (*laughing*). Na, na, I'm good.

JOEY raps and dances like he is drunk. He simmers down.

Astaghfirullah.

JOEY. I'm joking, bro. It's only apple juice.

JOEY shows him. It is apple juice.

OMZ. I can tell you're a lightweight anyways.

JOEY. Cap, if you ever drank, you'd be a lightweight yourself.

OMZ. We'll never know, 'cause I'll never be drinking.

JOEY. Did you speak to Lola? I told you she'd be there.

OMZ. I just said that her Js were hard and kept it moving.

JOEY. What did she say?

OMZ. 'Thanks.'

BILAL *and* JOEY. Ayy!!

JOEY. You're in bro!

OMZ. Also... she said I was funny?

JOEY. What?

OMZ. On a random one... I weren't even bussing any jokes.

BILAL. Swear down? Na you're definitely in – Ay!

BILAL and JOEY laugh.

OMZ. I was just confused, like...

BILAL. Jameela used to look nicer. (*Beat.*) Did you man see Zack as well? He got shook when he saw us.

OMZ. I was like, 'What's good?'

BILAL. And he was like, 'W-w-what's good bro?' He's still rattled from that primary school beating we gave him. Paigon!

They laugh. It dies down.

My dad would be fuming right now if he found out I went to a party.

OMZ. Bro he ain't gonna find out, he's at work alie? Then relax man. I know your dad can be a lot but it's cool man.

BILAL. Na, he's not a lot. He's just passionate. My dad was gonna make it, init. Leyton Orient wanted to sign him – but he had to pull out... had to look after family.

Pause.

And I didn't hear you man saying he was a lot it when he took us to Nando's after we won the District Cup.

OMZ. So long as you're enjoying what you're doing. That's the main thing.

BILAL. Yeah... I am.

Silence.

OMZ. Oh yeah, before I forget...

OMZ *takes off his Gucci belt and Prada side bag and gives it to* JOEY.

Love for that Joey.

JOEY. Light.

Beat.

BILAL. Next party, I'm just gonna take gyal to the archway and get their Snaps there.

OMZ. How many Snaps did you get?

BILAL. Three, but one Champions League babe didn't wanna give me her Snap 'cause she saw me asking two other girls. It got too bait.

OMZ. Next party, I'm defo gonna be bringing a munch back to Red Pitch. There was bare food in there. It's a howler from me not taking any.

BILAL *and* OMZ *laugh.*

JOEY. There ain't gonna be no next parties – not in that hall anyway.

BILAL. Oh, yeah, yeah... I hear that.

Beat.

JOEY. I got a number though – Alicia. I was talking to her properly; she was proper smart.

JOEY *nods, smiling as he reflects on his conversation with Alicia.* BILAL *and* OMZ *watch on.*

Ay Bilz, try and get a crib round my bit. I'll send you the address.

BILAL. Why?

JOEY. It'll be vibes. It'll basically be like living in Reedbury again… it's Liverpool Street Station sides.

OMZ. You're moving to Liverpool?

JOEY *walks towards the corner of Red Pitch.*

JOEY. It's near Liverpool Street Station, it's London – East London.

OMZ. Oh, calm. You said you're coming back though init?

JOEY. Where?

OMZ. To endz.

JOEY. Obviously.

JOEY*, in the corner of Red Pitch, is about to urinate until a consternated* OMZ *intervenes.*

OMZ. Ay, yo, yo, yo, what you doing?

JOEY *is confused by the question.*

What you doing man?

OMZ *shakes the cages of Red Pitch.*

JOEY. Ay, chill man.

OMZ. Are you mad? What you doing bruv?

JOEY. I'm pissing, what's your problem?

OMZ. Man are complaining 'bout endz 'changing', all our 'sick spots' being 'taken' and you're pissing in Red Pitch!?

JOEY (*sarcastically*). Yeah, it's my small, small piss that's ruined endz, that's why they have to change everything. (*Beat.*) Are you mad? It ain't got nothing to do with that. They leave it to get shegged on purpose so they can come in and change it.

OMZ *kisses his teeth.*

OMZ. All you have to do is look after your own endz, it ain't hard.

JOEY. How can you –

BILAL. Just leave it Joey. Piss outside. You can't say they've
    left endz to get mash-up but you're pissing in Red Pitch. It
    don't make no sense.

JOEY. I'm not even gonna say anything.

BILAL. Piss at your yard. We might as well cut, anyway.

OMZ. Yeah, for real. We need to get rest for them trials.

BILAL. 'Trials'? 'We'? Wait. Omz, you spoke to Coach?!
    Ayyyyy! Yes Omz, my guy!

JOEY. That's lit.

    BILAL *and* JOEY *nudge* OMZ.

BILAL. What did he say?

OMZ. I told him wagwarn with my grandad. He said there used
    to be a few people on endz that were young carers when he
    was growing up. He said he's gonna speak to them 'bout
    getting me help. I'm old enough so they won't split me and
    Rahim up.

BILAL. Calm. Shout us if you need any help as well.

    OMZ *nods – a restrained gratitude.*

OMZ. A good Muslim knows what forgiveness is.

BILAL (*still reeling with excitement*). Sunday is the day we
    change our lives boys!

OMZ. I prayed on it for all of us – InshāAllah!

JOEY. By the grace of Almighty God!

    *The boys exit Red Pitch pumped and excited, double-tapping
    the cage on their way out. The construction sounds rise in
    volume. After a moment, the construction returns to normal
    and sustains.*

Scene Six

A whistle blows. BILAL, JOEY *and* OMZ *are in a line on stage psyching themselves up. They speak with excitement and energy, whilst doing various drills but gradually it wanes and they become frustrated. It's explosive and intense supported by the lighting state and sound – there is no construction sound.*

OMZ. Have you heard anything?

BILAL. No, you?

OMZ. No, you?

JOEY. No.

   Reset.

OMZ. Yo, you heard anything?

BILAL. Na, you?

OMZ. Na, you?

JOEY. Na.

   Reset.

   Did you hear that donny from Eastside Rovers got scouted?

OMZ. Fammm, *you* heard anything?

BILAL. Na, you?

OMZ. Na man, what about you?

JOEY. Yeah.

Scene Seven

BILAL *and* OMZ *are in Red Pitch.* BILAL *is noticeably agitated whilst* OMZ *seems to be a lot more contained. The humming construction is more prominent than it's ever been.*

BILAL. I was badding it up, alie? Bare 'drop, drop' shoulders. Them scouts were getting so gassed. I saw them. They were clapping and everything.

OMZ. Where's Joey? We're meant to be playing FA no?

BILAL. And you know what's nuts? That dead Eastside Rovers left back got in. What's he got?

OMZ. Is Joey even coming?

BILAL. Joey said he'd be here in an hour.

OMZ. He said that an hour ago.

BILAL. Give him time init, he was unpacking. (*Beat.*) Didn't you see when I finessed it top bins. Like fam...

OMZ. He's taking his time.

BILAL. He said he's coming. Chill.

OMZ *shoots* BILAL *a 'who you talking to?' kind of look.*

When he gets here, we can do FA.

The construction sounds increase and intensify momentarily. For a moment, we hear audible chants: 'You should be ashamed, we don't want a change.' It then stabilises but still feels very intrusive.

What did your grandad say about trials?

OMZ. Psh.

BILAL *awaits his answer.*

Nothing.

BILAL. You didn't tell him?

OMZ (*agitated*). That I didn't get in?

BILAL. Yeah.

OMZ. Brudda, this guy don't even remember I went trials.

BILAL *shakes his head.*

BILAL. My dad didn't say anything, as well. I shouldn't have went to that party man.

OMZ. Joey went to that party and got in. You're supposed to have enjoyment when you're young. Listen, don't watch that man. There'll be other teams.

BILAL. Word. Deeping it, QPR ain't even all that.

OMZ *gives* BILAL *a glance.* BILAL *doesn't notice it.*

OMZ. Dial Joey man, this is dead.

BILAL. I have. Voicemail.

OMZ. When? Dial him again.

BILAL *phones* JOEY *reluctantly. It goes straight to voicemail. He puts it on speaker momentarily before locking it off.*

Brudda, I'm due to cut, this is –

BILAL. No man, not yet. We ain't done Joey's farewell match.

OMZ. He's not coming. You're holding / on.

BILAL. He said he was / coming.

OMZ. How many man said they're coming, when they move, they don't turn up?

BILAL. Joey will come back.

The construction sounds intensify. OMZ *becomes visibly frustrated, acknowledging the construction for the first time,* BILAL *acknowledges it too, they share a worried look.*

I spoke to Coach.

OMZ. What did he say?

BILAL. Talking 'bout the real trials are how we bounce back from this, responding to disappointment.

OMZ *shakes his head*. JOEY *enters, ritualistically double-tapping the cage.*

JOEY. Yo!

BILAL. Told you he was coming.

JOEY. What you man saying? Fam, these buses take the longest. Next time, I'm gonna take bike.

Pause.

I'm here for my FA farewell. (*Beat.*) You man, I have the pengest neighbour. I think she's digging your boy. Every time she sees me, she's always smiling at me...

BILAL.... Yeah?

JOEY. Yeahhh fammm. I'm chatting to Alicia, though. Trust me Bilz, when you get out of this estate, you're gonna find bare new gyal.

OMZ *shoots* JOEY *a cold glance.*

BILAL. Congrats on getting scouted.

OMZ. What happens now?

JOEY. Scholarship. I start off with the under-seventeens then they're gonna move me to the under-eighteens... then if I do good: pro contract.

BILAL *and* OMZ *are not as happy for* JOEY *as he expects.*

They'll be paying me like five bills a month on the under-eighteens you know.

Silence.

The scout was saying they got bare players in the team like you man.

BILAL. What? He spoke 'bout us yeah?

OMZ. What did he say?

JOEY. Yeah... well not like you lot... but the people that didn't get in. It's 'cause they have players in the team like you lot already.

BILAL. Oh.

   Beat.

JOEY. FA. Come. Not in goal.

OMZ. What? You're a goalkeeper though.

JOEY. Yeah. I don't feel like going in goal today.

BILAL. You always go in goal.

JOEY. I don't wanna go in goal today though.

OMZ. Bro, just go in –

BILAL. I'll go in goal. It's calm.

   BILAL *walks over to the goal. Construction sounds.* OMZ
   shoots JOEY *a cold glance.* BILAL *kicks the ball out.* JOEY
   barges OMZ *to the ground.* JOEY *has the ball at his feet.*
   OMZ, *evidently carrying anger, gets up, charges towards*
   JOEY *and flies into him, leaving him on the ground.* JOEY
   rolls in pain.

JOEY. What you doing?!!

OMZ. Accident.

JOEY. Bruv, you didn't even go for the ball!

OMZ. It was an accident init…

BILAL. What's your problem?!

OMZ. Are you deaf?!! Accident!!

BILAL. No it weren't.

OMZ. Whatever. Are you alright Joey?

JOEY. My ankle is finished.

BILAL. Move man!

OMZ. Move Bilal – am I talking to you?!!! You're always
   trying to be Superman. Move!!!!

JOEY. You man chill.

BILAL. Wasteman.

OMZ. You're a wasteman.

BILAL. You're moving dumb. You're gonna be alone. You're a loner. Get over it.

OMZ. I'll bang you in your face right now, soft yout. Shut your mouth!

JOEY. Ayyy, calm down you man!

BILAL. Do it then! You're sour. Always talking 'bout 'back in the day, back in the day'. Move on you loser.

OMZ. Shut your mouth you prick. You're mad you never got in. You're a failure just like your dad.

BILAL. Shut the fuck up, with your 'Ah, they're renewing the endz.', 'It's gonna be good for my grandad', 'Lifts gonna be working for my grandad.' No one gives a fuck about your grandad.

OMZ punches BILAL aggressively in his face. It escalates.

Am I dickhead?!

JOEY. Oi, chill you man!!

OMZ. Do something then!

BILAL pushes OMZ. OMZ punches BILAL in his face sending BILAL to the ground. BILAL gets up. They swing for each other, head locking, punching and kicking. This fight should feel explosive. Intense. After a moment, they stop. BILAL's nose is bleeding. He's also crying.

Soft. Why you crying for?

BILAL. Dickhead.

OMZ. You're a dickhead.

BILAL. Ay. Come Joey.

BILAL is visibly riled.

Pass my ball…

OMZ. Take your ball.

OMZ *kicks the ball outside of the pitch.*

JOEY *limps out with his arm around* BILAL.

BILAL *leaves Red Pitch but instead of double-tapping the cage ritualistically,* BILAL *wipes his blood on the wall. A moment to be marked – horror, terror, danger. The sound of construction increases, the chants of 'You should be ashamed, we don't want a change' rumble underneath until all sound diminuendos to just the construction.*

Scene Eight

OMZ *is in Red Pitch by himself with his deflated football. He is pushing himself as much as he can. After a moment,* BILAL *enters with his football and* OMZ *stiffens his back, bracing himself.* BILAL, *without looking at* OMZ, *goes to the other side of Red Pitch and practises. He takes out his cones and begins to place them down in Red Pitch.*

OMZ *watches* BILAL *set up his cones. He then leaves.* BILAL *watches him go and then he takes out his phone, places it on the wall and then speaks to it.*

BILAL. Hey everyone, my name is Bilal Amaral – sixteen years old – welcome to my YouTube channel.

He does an explosive sprint on the spot.

He goes back to working hard with the football but realising the camera is not following him, he sighs, stops practising and then stops filming himself.

Can't even see.

BILAL *exits.*

The construction sounds continue.

Scene Nine

JOEY *is in Red Pitch in his QPR kit with* OMZ. OMZ *assesses* JOEY*'s ankle, he's really apologetic.* JOEY *acknowledges* OMZ*'s sorrow and gives a forgiving thumbs-up. A reconciling moment.*

JOEY. So what? You man are never gonna chat to each other again?

OMZ. When he says sorry init.

JOEY. What if he doesn't say sorry?

OMZ. He's moving anyway. He'll do his thing and I'll do mine.

JOEY. What you gonna do?

Beat.

It's silly now man. You and Bilz – it's silly.

OMZ. I didn't –

JOEY. I don't even care Omz. It's just dumb...

BILAL *enters. He notices* OMZ *talking to* JOEY *and hides his surprise. He wasn't expecting him to be here.*

BILAL. Wagwarn Joey.

JOEY. What you saying Bilz?

BILAL *nudges* JOEY, *pretending that* OMZ *doesn't exist.* OMZ *shakes his head and goes off to play on one end of the pitch with his deflated ball whilst* BILAL *plays on the other side.*

I called you man so we can do my farewell init.

Silence.

Since we weren't able to finish it up last time.

Silence.

BILAL. What's QPR saying?

JOEY. It's calm... I was speaking to the kit lady and I started deeping it – without you man, I wouldn't have got in.

BILAL *and* OMZ *both look at* JOEY.

She was asking me how did I get so good, did I have special training… I was like na, I just played Sunday League and kicked ball with my boys. Who knows if I would've done the Sunday League thing if it weren't for you man. All them times you lot shouted me to come Red Pitch. Putting me in goal. You man trained me up.

BILAL *and* OMZ *look at each other and then quickly look away.* JOEY *is disappointed. A moment passes.*

OMZ (*to* BILAL). I see you're doing the YouTube thing.

BILAL, *after a moment, realises* OMZ *is talking to him.* JOEY *is hopeful.*

BILAL. Yeah.

OMZ. Yeah, that's hard.

BILAL *ignores* OMZ.

You got bare followers too.

BILAL *nods.*

Silence.

BILAL. You seen the pics from Jameela's party?

OMZ, *about to respond, sees that* BILAL *is talking directly to* JOEY.

JOEY. Yeah, seen them on her Insta. That one with all three of us looks too sick. Omz you were flexing in that Gucci belt!

BILAL. The one of me and you was cold.

JOEY *looks on at* BILAL, *frustrated.*

Beat.

JOEY. Are we playing or…? I've gotta leave soon. I need to skip that rush-hour. I'm due to get that 'home-time' call if it gets too late.

JOEY *forces a laugh but* OMZ *ignores* JOEY. *After a moment,* OMZ *exits, leaving his deflated ball behind.*

Pattern up Bilal man!

BILAL. Me?!

JOEY. Yeah, pattern up! What's the point of me coming back to endz and you man ain't talking?

BILAL. Bro, what's the new area saying?

JOEY. Ay Bilal –

BILAL. I told my parents about bidding around your sides.

JOEY. Listen to me for a sec–

BILAL. It's an option init.

JOEY. Listen to me bruv!! Squash it with Omz before we start college. Or trust me, we'll all just… drift apart. We ain't gonna be on Reedbury.

BILAL. I'm glad I ain't gonna be on Reedbury.

JOEY. You should just apologise. I know it's cutting you up. That's the one donny that always had your back. Always.

BILAL *has no defence.*

(*Firmly.*) Just be the bigger man.

JOEY *exits, leaving* BILAL *in Red Pitch alone.*

OMZ *re-enters, there's an urgency.* BILAL *doesn't acknowledge* OMZ. OMZ *thinks about speaking to* BILAL, *he hesitates, then he leaves.* BILAL *turns back as* OMZ *exits, he sighs. Suddenly* OMZ *returns.*

OMZ. You seen my grandad?

BILAL. What?

OMZ. Have you seen my grandad? Rahim said he left the house time ago and he ain't come back since.

BILAL. Swear down? Na I ain't seen him.

OMZ. Could Rahim stay at yours for a bit – 'cause he's already been alone for too long? And I need to look for grandad.

BILAL. Definitely, let's drop him at mine and I'll help you look.

BILAL *and* OMZ *hurriedly exit.*

Scene Ten

BILAL *enters Red Pitch. He practises.* OMZ *enters, he's dressed casually. He has an unopened tropical juice and Twix which he hands to* BILAL.

OMZ. Here, take.

BILAL *is surprised but takes it. He opens it and glances at* OMZ. *He takes one bar of the Twix and then he hands* OMZ *the other.* OMZ *is reluctant at first.*

BILAL. Trust me, it's calm.

OMZ *takes it and eats it. A moment of silence hangs in Red Pitch – it is a comfortable silence as they both enjoy their Twix bar.*

You took Joey out differently.

BILAL *chuckles.* OMZ *confused at first joins in.*

OMZ. It was an acci– I didn't mean it.

They share a light-hearted chuckle.

BILAL. If I was on the pitch, I probably would've done something similar myself.

They chuckle.

I don't even know what I'm doing next Omz. It was football for me.

OMZ. You got options. Obviously, results day soon – you ain't dumb. But like... there's football college, there's the online thing, there's tournaments. It's up to you.

BILAL. Mmm. I don't even know. At the moment, I can't even tell what I want to do or what I'm being forced to do.

OMZ *nods*.

Silence.

OMZ (*struggling to say it*). Yeah... thank you... for... with my grandad.

BILAL. That's what family are for, my bro. I'm just glad he's good, Alhamdullilah.

OMZ. Alhamdullilah.

They share a glance, a mutual exchange of respect.

BILAL. I spoke to my dad... I told him that I need to have more of a balance.

OMZ. What did he say?

BILAL. He said, 'Balance? Which balance?'

BILAL *chuckles*.

OMZ. It's good to have someone that cares though. (*Beat*.) Sorry about scrapping... I didn't mean to... And love for the help again... I –

BILAL. It's calm bro... It's all love. Even when I'm gone just shout me.

Silence.

OMZ. Ay Bilz, I'm moving you know.

BILAL *looks at* OMZ.

Yeah, we gotta go ASAP 'cause of my grandad. He needs adapted accommodation. The new flats won't be ready in time. The new spot's closer to a hospital as well – I'm gonna need support.

BILAL. What? Wait. So you're leaving Reedbury?

OMZ *is quiet, trying to be 'strong'*.

I don't believe you... You being serious?...

OMZ *wipes away a tear.*

When do you go then?

OMZ. Next weekend, still…

BILAL. That's… swear?

Silence.

OMZ. I thought them renewing endz would've been lit: everyone still local, endz sparkly, my grandad would be calm but…

BILAL. Mmmm.

Silence.

JOEY *enters.*

JOEY. Ay, you man seen Esme's dry cleaner's is boarded up, it's crazy.

BILAL. What you doing round these sides?

BILAL *and* JOEY *share a chuckle.*

JOEY. Omz messaged, said you man'll be around.

BILAL *looks at* OMZ.

BILAL. Omz is leaving Reedbury.

JOEY. What?! When?!

OMZ. Next weekend, still.

JOEY. Why?!

OMZ. My grandad, still.

JOEY. Damn.

Silence.

Damn. Imagine, this was where we all met… Ay Omz, you gonna come back to Red Pitch?

OMZ. Definitely.

JOEY. Imagine if they try close it.

BILAL. Never, I'll slap their heads.

They laugh.

JOEY. So what now?

BILAL *shrugs*.

You wanna do a farewell game? (*Beat*.) Omz?

OMZ. Come. FA. Red Pitch rules.

JOEY *goes in goal*. BILAL *and* OMZ *take a moment to warm into the game but get going*. OMZ *does a 'drop, drop' shoulder and goes round* BILAL *and scores*.

BILAL. Using my moves now, yeah?

OMZ. 'Drop, drop' shoulder – easy!

BILAL. Cool. Come.

OMZ. Na, I'm done bro, I'm retiring as champ.

BILAL. But you didn't win.

OMZ. Who scored more goals?

BILAL. Best out of three.

OMZ. Na, na. I'm hungry as well.

JOEY. We can walk down to Camberwell, get some Morley's?

OMZ. Come.

OMZ *and* JOEY *exit, double-tapping the cage ritualistically as they leave.*

(*Offstage*.) Ay, Bilz!

BILAL. I'm coming, one sec.

BILAL *picks up his ball. He puts the deflated ball in the centre circle of Red Pitch.*

OMZ *and* JOEY *re-enter.*

OMZ. Ay, brudda?

BILAL *takes a picture of the deflated ball. The boys then form a huddle in the centre circle. After a moment, they break out of the huddle and then exit, double-tapping the cage.*

Spotlight on deflated ball in centre circle. Crescendo of construction sounds.

Lights and sound snap out.

End.

Bush Theatre

We make theatre for London. Now.

For over 50 years the Bush Theatre has been a world-famous home for new plays, internationally renowned as 'the place to go for ground-breaking work as diverse as its audiences' (Evening Standard).

Combining meaningful community engagement work with industry leading talent development schemes and ambitious artistic programming, the Bush Theatre champions and supports unheard voices to develop the artists and audiences of the future. As a charity, this work is made possible thanks to vital support from a community of generous donors, supporters and trusts who are responsible for raising a third of the Bush's annual income.

Since its early days in a small room above a pub on the corner of Shepherd's Bush Green and now in its new home at the beautifully renovated old library just around the corner, the Bush has produced more than 500 ground-breaking premieres of new plays. They have nurtured the careers of writers including Simon Stephens, Temi Wilkey, James Graham, Lucy Kirkwood, Arinzé Kene, Ambreen Razia, Jonathan Harvey and Jack Thorne, and launched actors including Alan Rickman, Victoria Wood, Julie Walters, Ronkẹ Adékoluẹjo, Cush Jumbo, Andrew Scott and Phoebe Waller-Bridge into the mainstream.

Recent successes include multi-award-winning productions *Red Pitch* by Tyrell Williams, *Lava* by Benedict Lombe, *Sleepova* by Matilda Feyiṣayọ Ibini, *Invisible* by Nikhil Parmar and *Misty* by Arinzé Kene. Richard Gadd's *Baby Reindeer*, Igor Memic's *Old Bridge*, and Waleed Akhtar's *The P Word* won the Olivier Award for 'Outstanding Achievement in an Affiliate Theatre' in 2021, 2022 and 2023 respectively. In 2023 the Bush won The Stage's 'Theatre of the Year' award and produced Sir Lenny Henry's first play *August in England*.

In 2024, the Bush's Artistic Director Lynette Linton, Executive Director Mimi Findlay and Associate Artistic Director Daniel Bailey were included in The Stage 100 list of the most influential people in theatre, recognising the scale of the impact the Bush Theatre continues to have.

bushtheatre.co.uk
@bushtheatre

Bush Theatre

MAKING A LASTING IMPACT ON THE FUTURE OF NEW WRITING

The Bush Theatre would like to thank all its supporters whose valuable contributions have helped us to create a platform for our future. Their support enables us to promote the highest quality new writing, develop the next generation of creative talent, lead innovative community engagement work and champion diversity.

There are many ways you can support the Bush Theatre. Becoming a Star Supporter is the perfect way to build a relationship with us and get unrivalled access to the theatre and artists, you can become a Friend, leave us a gift in your will or give us a one off donation. **Find out more: bushtheatre.co.uk/support-us**

Bush Theatre, 7 Uxbridge Road, London W12 8LJ
Box Office: 020 8743 5050 | Administration: 020 8743 3584
Email: info@bushtheatre.co.uk | bushtheatre.co.uk

Alternative Theatre Company Ltd
The Bush Theatre is a Registered Charity
and a company limited by guarantee.
Registered in England no. 1221968 Charity no. 270080

www.nickhernbooks.co.uk

facebook.com/nickhernbooks

twitter.com/nickhernbooks